AF870582

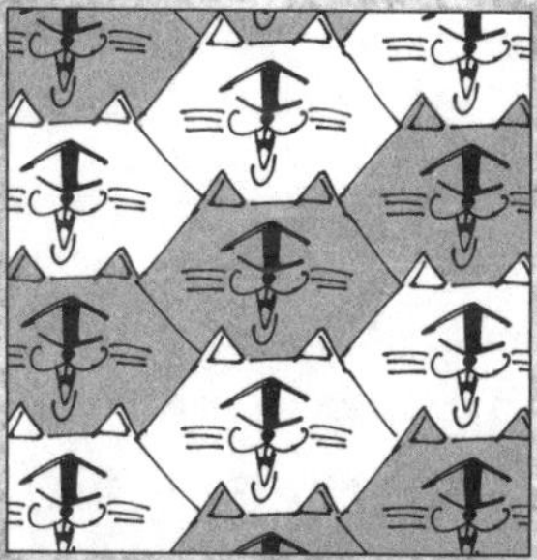

GEGE AKUTAMI

Come out and fight!
Come out and fiiight!

GEGE AKUTAMI published a few short works before starting *Jujutsu Kaisen*, which began serialization in *Weekly Shonen Jump* in 2018.

JUJUTSU KAISEN

VOLUME 9
SHONEN JUMP MANGA EDITION

BY GEGE AKUTAMI

TRANSLATION Stefan Koza
TOUCH-UP ART & LETTERING Snir Aharon
DESIGN Joy Zhang
EDITOR John Bae
CONSULTING EDITOR Erika Onabe

JUJUTSU KAISEN © 2018 by Gege Akutami
All rights reserved.
First published in Japan in 2018 by SHUEISHA Inc., Tokyo.
English translation rights arranged by SHUEISHA Inc.

The stories, characters and incidents mentioned
in this publication are entirely fictional.

No portion of this book may be reproduced
or transmitted in any form or by any means without
written permission from the copyright holders.

Printed in the U.S.A.

Published by VIZ Media, LLC
P.O. Box 77010
San Francisco, CA 94107

18
First printing, April 2021
Eighteenth printing, April 2026

VIZ MEDIA
viz.com

SHONEN JUMP

ratings.viz.com RATED T+ OLDER TEEN

PARENTAL ADVISORY
JUJUTSU KAISEN is rated T+ for Older Teen and is recommended for ages 16 and up. This volume contains fantasy violence.

JUJUTSU KAISEN

9

PREMATURE DEATH

STORY AND ART BY GEGE AKUTAMI

JUJUTSU KAISEN
CAST OF CHARACTERS

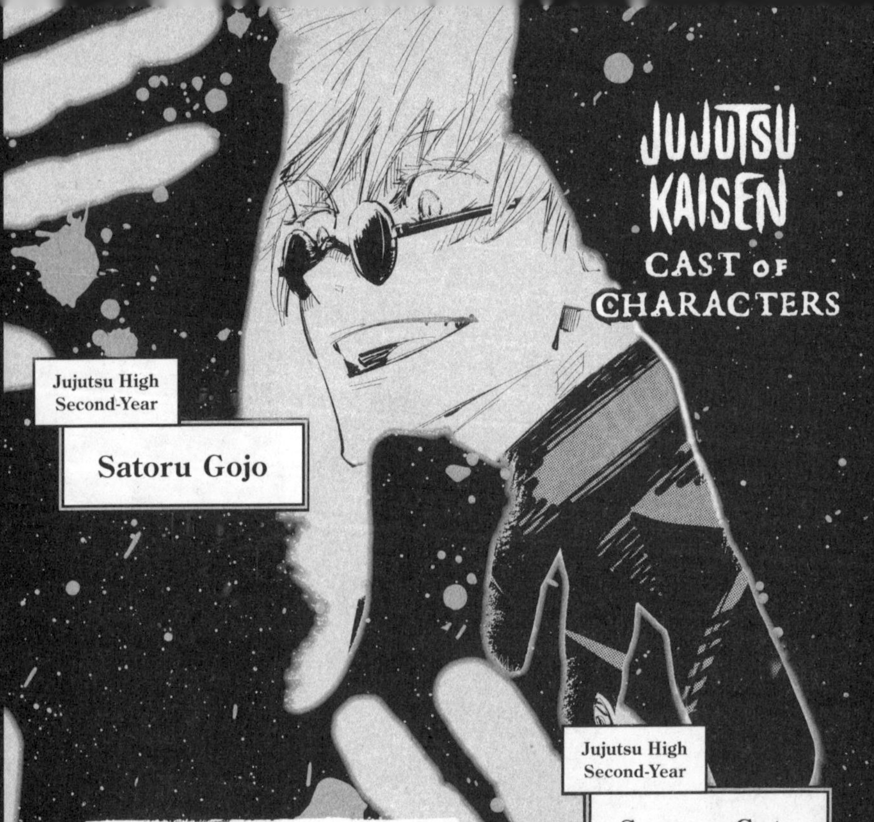

—CURSE—

Hardship, regret, shame... The misery that comes from these negative human emotions can lead to death.

Itadori and Kugisaki manage to defeat two of the three Curse Womb: Death Paintings and retrieve a Sukuna finger. The story then flashes back to Satoru Gojo's time as a second-year at Jujutsu High. He and fellow student Suguru Geto are sent on a mission to retrieve a girl named Riko Amanai for Master Tengen. Master Tengen's rapidly evolving body must merge with a fresh vessel known as the Plasma Star Vessel, and Riko's the perfect match. However, there are interested parties who will do anything to prevent this merger...

Jujutsu High
Second-Year
Shoko Ieiri
Grade 1
Jujutsu Sorcerer
Masamichi Yaga
Star Plasma
Vessel
Riko Amanai
Sorcerer Killer
Toji Fushiguro

JUJUTSU KAISEN

9

PREMATURE DEATH

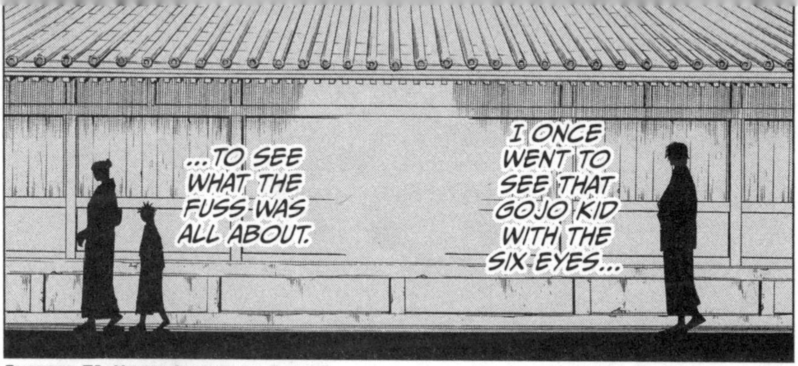

CHAPTER 71: HIDDEN INVENTORY, PART 7

THAT'S WHY I WAITED UNTIL YOU WERE WORN DOWN.
Chapter 71: Hidden Inventory, Part 7
VOON
VWAM
VWOOM

CHOMP
SATO-RU!
FWP

IT'S FINE.
I DIDN'T CAST MY CURSED TECHNIQUE IN TIME, BUT HE DIDN'T HIT ANY VITAL ORGANS.
AND I REINFORCED MY CURSED ENERGY TO MAKE SURE THE SWORD DIDN'T DO ANY FURTHER DAMAGE.
KRSSHT
KINDA LIKE A SAFETY PIN GOING THROUGH A KNITTED SWEATER.
REALLY, I'M GOOD.
AMANAI IS THE PRIORITY. I'LL TAKE CARE OF THIS.
GET TO MASTER TENGEN'S PLACE QUICKLY.

JOLT
DON'T LET YOUR GUARD DOWN.
WHO DO YA THINK YOU'RE TALKIN' TO?
VLUSH

IT'S A DIFFERENT SWORD THAN BEFORE...
AND WHERE'D THAT CURSED SPIRIT WRAPPED AROUND HIS BODY COME FROM?

VWFOOM
DAMMIT! WHAT'S GOING ON?!
I WAS HOPING TO FINISH YOU OFF WITH THAT STRIKE.
MUST BE GETTING RUSTY.
WHERE'D THE STAR PLASMA VESSEL GO?
AMANAI'S BOUNTY HAS ALREADY BEEN LIFTED, YOU IDIOT.
YEAH, BECAUSE I TOOK IT DOWN, MR. HOTSHOT.
IT WAS HILARIOUS THAT YOU GUYS WENT TO OKINAWA THOUGH.
TO GAIN AN ADVANTAGE OVER GUYS AS TIGHTLY GUARDED AS YOU, I CREATED THE ILLUSION OF ACHIEVING YOUR GOALS.
IT'S REGRETTABLE THAT NONE OF THE SORCERERS WITH YOU DIED, BUT IF THERE WASN'T ANY TIME LIMIT ON THE BOUNTY...
Renchoku Girls' Junior High second-year Wanted dead or alive.
Time Left:
47:40:56
$ 250,00
...YOU PROBABLY WOULDN'T HAVE STOPPED YOUR TECHNIQUE UNTIL THE END.

IS THAT RIGHT?
VOON

VOON
VOON
VOON
VWAM

FWIP
!
HE'S NOT JUST FAST. I KNEW THERE WAS SOMETHING WEIRD ABOUT THIS GUY...
HE HAS ZERO CURSED ENERGY! IT'S ALL INNATE PHYSICAL PROWESS!
GLUP
I CAN'T READ HIS MOVES!!

DUN
DUN
DUN

WHAM
VREE
HE KNOWS ABOUT MY CURSED TECHNIQUE. THAT'S WHY HE LAYS LOW. HE HAS TO HAVE A PLAN. IT MUST INVOLVE THAT CURSED TOOL HE JUST TOOK OUT.
IS THAT YOUR SECRET WEAPON? TOO BAD YOU CAN'T GET CLOSE ENOUGH TO USE IT.
!
WHERE IS HE?!

TP...
TP TP...
FSH FSH...
I CAN'T SENSE HIM WITHOUT CURSED ENERGY. SHOULD I RELY ON INSTINCT?
NO, I'LL TRY TO SENSE THE ENERGY OF THAT CURSED SPIRIT WRAPPED AROUND HIM.
HOW'S HE SO FAST?!
CURSED TECH-NIQUE LAPSE
GOT NO CHOICE!
MAXIMUM CURSED ENERGY OUTPUT

BLUE

GA GA

FWSH
NOW THERE'S NOTHING IN THE WAY TO BLOCK MY VIEW. NO MORE SURPRISE ATTACKS.
HIDING IN THE FOREST?
VWWWWW
!
THOSE ARE...

FLY HEADS ?!
KSHH KS HH KSHH
THEY WERE STORED INSIDE OF THAT CURSED SPIRIT.
I SEE, USING THEM LIKE A CHAFF GRENADE.
I CAN'T LOCATE HIM, AND MY VIEW IS BLOCKED AGAIN. I'LL USE BLUE...
NO, BUT HIS TARGET IS...

AMA-NAI—
THE SHARP INSTINCT THAT CAN DETECT ME EVEN WHEN UNARMED!
WITH YOUR SIX EYES, YOU CAN SEE THE FOREIGN CURSED ENERGY THAT FLOWS OUT OF THIS CURSED TOOL. YOU DON'T WANT TO LET IT GET CLOSE.
SO NOW YOU'RE FINALLY ON THE DEFENSIVE.

SPECIAL GRADE CURSED TOOL: INVERTED SPEAR OF HEAVEN

ITS EFFECT: FORCED STOPPAGE OF A CURSED TECHNIQUE

• When unregistered cursed energy is detected within Jujutsu High's barrier, an alarm goes off.

• For this reason, Geto is normally prohibited from using his cursed technique on Jujutsu High's campus.

• Because Geto's such an exemplary student, whenever he needs to use his cursed technique, he'll inform the school beforehand. However, he sometimes gets into fights with Gojo and uses it without permission.

↖ Isn't this a convenient way of using his technique?

Special Grade Cursed Tool: Inverted Spear of Heaven

Chapter 72: Hidden Inventory, Part 8

SHp
GPK GPK

SHUK
SHUK
SHUK

RUK
SPLAT
I'M STARTING TO...
...REMEMBER HOW TO DO THIS.

GWONG
GWONG
AT THE BOTTOM OF JUJUTSU HIGH
TOMBS OF THE STAR CORRIDOR
KRSHHH
MASTER RIKO.

THIS IS AS FAR AS I GO.
MASTER RIKO, PLEASE TAKE...
FSH
KUROI!
I LOVE YOU!
SKWEEZ

ALWAYS!
NOW AND FOR-EVER!!
I-I LOVE YOU TOO...!
IS THIS...?
YES.

WE'RE JUST OUTSIDE OF WHERE MASTER TENGEN RESIDES...
THIS IS THE COUNTRY'S BASE FOR PRIMARY BARRIERS...

THE MAIN HALL OF THE TOMBS OF THE STAR CORRIDOR!

GO DOWN THE STAIRS AND PASS THE GATE.
THEN HEAD TOWARD THE BASE OF THAT HUGE TREE.
IT'S PRO-TECTED BY A DIFFERENT BARRIER THAN THE ONE AROUND JUJUTSU HIGH.
ONLY THOSE INVITED MAY ENTER.
YOU'LL BE PROTECTED BY MASTER TENGEN UNTIL THE MERGER.
OR YOU CAN TURN BACK...
...AND RETURN HOME WITH KUROI.

...
WHAT?
WHEN WE WERE ASSIGNED THIS MISSION BY OUR TEACHER...
...HE REFERRED TO THE MERGER AS AN "ERASURE."
IT'S AS IF HE LOOKED AT IT AS SOMETHING WRONG.
FOR A MUSCLE-BRAINED GUY LIKE HIM, HE LIKES TO BEAT AROUND THE BUSH.
SATORU AND I BOTH CAME TO A DECISION BEFORE WE MET YOU.
KLINK
IF THE KID WHO IS THE STAR PLASMA VESSEL SHOULD REFUSE THE MERGER...

...
THEN WE CALL IT OFF!
HEH HEH HEH...
YOU SURE ABOUT THAT?
HUH?
WE MIGHT HAVE TO FIGHT MASTER TENGEN.
YOU SCARED?
DON'T WORRY! WE SHOULD BE FINE.

WE'RE...
...THE STRONGEST.
NO MATTER WHAT YOU CHOOSE...
...WE PROMISE TO PROTECT YOUR FUTURE.
...
I...

EVER SINCE I WAS BORN, I'VE BEEN TOLD THAT I'M SPECIAL AND DIFFERENT.
BEING SPECIAL WAS NORMAL FOR ME.
I'VE SURVIVED TILL NOW BY STAYING AWAY FROM DANGER.
MY PARENTS DIED IN A CAR CRASH.
I DON'T REMEM-BER IT.
I'M NOT SAD OR LONELY ANYMORE.
THAT'S WHY...
...WITH THE MERGER, I THOUGHT I'D BE OKAY...
...LEAVING EVERYONE.
NO MATTER HOW PAINFUL IT BECAME, I BELIEVED THAT...
...SOME-DAY...
...THE SADNESS AND LONELINESS WOULD DISAPPEAR.

BUT...
BUT NOW...
I WANT TO...
...STAY WITH EVERYONE A BIT LONGER.
I WANT TO GO TO MORE PLACES AND SEE MORE THINGS WITH EVERYONE...
MORE!!
RIKO...
LET'S GO HOME.

YEAH!
SHP

RIKO?
ALL RIGHT, GOOD SHOW.
TIME TO WRAP THINGS UP NOW.
HOW...
HOW'D YOU GET HERE?
HOW ...?
OH, GOTCHA.

I KILLED SATORU GOJO.
I SEE...
KRAK
KRAK
KRAK

THEN DIE!
KRAK
KRAK

¥500,000,000

THE TOMBS OF THE STAR AND THE CURSED WAREHOUSE ARE BARRIERS FOR *HIDING.*
YOU CAN'T LEAVE GUARDS AT THE ENTRANCE.
SO AS LONG AS YOU KNOW WHERE THE ENTRANCE IS LOCATED, THERE SHOULD BE NO PROBLEMS FINDING IT.
JUJUTSU SORCERERS ARE BUSY AROUND THIS TIME OF YEAR.
PLUS, FLY HEADS HAVE INFESTED THE SCHOOL AND THINGS ARE HECTIC OUTSIDE.
AS SOME-ONE WHO POSSESSES NO CURSED ENERGY, I'M THE INVISIBLE MAN.
BUT THERE IS ONE PROBLEM...
AS SOON AS I HOLD A CURSED TOOL, THE CURSED ENERGY FROM IT...
...MEANS I AM NO LONGER INVISIBLE.
CHAPTER 73: HIDDEN INVENTORY, PART 9

WHOA, SLOW DOWN.
BLAM
BLAM
BLAM

VWOOM
KRCH
KRCH
KRCH

GRRAK
LET ME CONTINUE.
YOU SEE, I'VE GOT THIS CURSED SPIRIT THAT CAN STORE OBJECTS.
I USE IT TO CARRY MY CURSED TOOLS.
NOW I KNOW WHAT YOU'RE THINKING... SHOULDN'T THE CURSED ENERGY...
...FROM THE SPIRIT MAKE HIM VISIBLE?!

BLECH
THE SPIRIT SHRINKS BY STORING ITSELF WITHIN ITS OWN BODY.
THEN I INGEST IT AND KEEP IT INSIDE MY STOMACH.
AN INVISIBLE MAN'S GONNA HAVE INVISIBLE GUTS, RIGHT?
THAT'S WHY I CAN MOVE THROUGH BARRIERS WHILE CARRYING CURSED TOOLS!
VLP
LUP LUP
AND THAT'S WHY I DIDN'T USE A CURSED TOOL AT FIRST.
I NEED TO STAY INVISIBLE IF I'M GONNA PULL OFF A SURPRISE ATTACK ON THE SIX EYES.

I COULD HAVE STARTED WITH THE STAR PLASMA VESSEL.
BUT IT'S RISKY TO REVEAL MYSELF TO THE SIX EYES.
BLECH
SHUT UP!
IT'S HEAVENLY RESTRICTION, RIGHT?!
LIKE US, REVEALING CERTAIN INFORMATION...
...CAN ACTUALLY GIVE YOU AN ADVANTAGE. I GET THAT.
THAT'S NOT WHAT I WANT TO KNOW.
HOW DID YOU KNOW ABOUT THE ENTRANCE INTO THE TOMBS?
WE MADE SURE TO NOT LEAVE ANY *RESIDUALS* BEHIND.
HUMANS LEAVE BEHIND MORE THAN JUST CURSED ENERGY, REMEMBER?
ODOR AND FOOTPRINTS, FOR EXAMPLE.
MY FIVE SENSES ARE SHARP THANKS TO MY LACK OF CURSED ENERGY.

THERE SHOULD'VE BEEN ONE MORE LADY ALONG THE WAY.
WHERE IS SHE?
HUH?
OH, YOU MEAN THE MAID?
PROBABLY DEAD.
I DIDN'T REALLY CARE IF SHE SURVIVED OR NOT.
IF SHE'S LUCKY, SHE'S ALIVE.
I SEE. THAT SETTLES IT.
DIE!
WOOM

VWP

BOOF
KSHH
HE CUT IT OPEN?!
THE RAINBOW DRAGON HAS THE HARDEST SKIN OF ALL MY CURSED SPIRITS!
CURSE MANIPULATION...
JUST A BUNCH OF RABBLE.
HEY.

AM...
AM...
AM I...
... PRETTY?
AN IMAGINARY VENGEFUL SPIRIT... AN INNATE DOMAIN WITH A PACT THAT CANNOT BE BROKEN UNTIL THE QUESTION IS ANSWERED.
WELL...
LET'S SEE.
YOU LOOK INTERESTING, BUT...
YOU'RE NOT MY TYPE.

KREEK
KRINK
FWSH
DRIP

SO, THAT'S HOW IT IS.
FTINK
FTINK
!!
FWOOP

IDIOT... COMING IN CLOSE AGAINST ME? YOU'VE GOT NO CHANCE.
THIS IS THE END.
FOR YOU!
FLOOP FLOOP
!

CURSE MANIPULATION...
A CURSED TECHNIQUE THAT ALLOWS ONE TO CONTROL CONQUERED CURSED SPIRITS.
IF THE DIFFERENCE IN LEVEL IS TWO OR MORE, ONE CAN TAKE IN A CURSED SPIRIT WITH PRACTICALLY NO CONDITIONS ATTACHED.
SOR-CERER
SPECIAL
1ST
2ND
3RD
4TH
SPIRIT
SPECIAL
1ST
2ND
3RD
4TH
HIS ABILITY MAY BE SPECIAL, BUT THE CURSED SPIRIT ITSELF IS NOT THAT STRONG. I CAN TAKE IT!
I'VE ELIMI-NATED THE WEAPONS CACHE.
NOW I'LL USE PHYSICAL...
KRCH
...ATTACKS!

WHAT?!
MY ATTACK WAS REPELLED ?!
BLECH
SHI
NG

VWIP

KRSHH
YOU'RE A SORCERER. YOU'LL BE FINE.
BOOF
I WOULD'VE KILLED YA IF YOU WERE A SHIKIGAMI USER.
BUT SINCE YOU'RE A CURSE MANIPULATOR...
...I DUNNO WHAT'LL HAPPEN WITH THE CURSES YOU'VE TAKEN IN IF YOU DIE.
I'D RATHER AVOID THE TROUBLE FOR NOW.
WHAK
BE SURE TO THANK YOUR PARENTS.

BUT YOU GUYS, WITH ALL YOUR BLESSED TALENTS...
...LOST TO A MONKEY LIKE ME WHO CAN'T EVEN USE JUJUTSU.

DON'T YOU DARE FORGET THAT IF YOU WANNA LIVE A LONG LIFE.
OH... I REMEMBER NOW.
MEGUMI. THE NAME MEANS "BLESSINGS."
AND I'M THE ONE WHO GAVE HIM THAT NAME.
TWITCH

△ The reason Geto couldn't absorb the weapon cache is that Papa-guro had already established a master-servant relationship with it. What follows, as far as this is concerned, becomes apparent in volume 0.

◁ I first thought Papa-guro's response was a bit gentle, but then I remembered he's a pro at freeloading off women, so I left it as is.

STAR RELIGIOUS GROUP HEADQUARTERS
HOUSE OF THE CHILDREN OF THE STAR
CHAPTER 74: HIDDEN INVENTORY, PART 10

HERE YOU GO.
GLORP

THUD
THE CORPSE OF THE STAR PLASMA VESSEL, RIKO AMANAI.
ALL IN ONE PIECE.

HM...
INDEED.
STAR RELIGIOUS GROUP REPRESENTATIVE SHIGERU SONODA
YOU'LL RECEIVE YOUR MONEY THROUGH THE MEANS WE PREVIOUSLY DISCUSSED.
WE'LL ADD ON A LITTLE EXTRA FOR YOUR TROUBLES.
HOW KIND OF YOU, MISTER FOUNDING FATHER.
REALLY? EVEN IF IT WAS A NECESSARY EXPENSE, HE GOT A LOT OF HELP FROM YOU.
HE'S NOT THE FOUNDER.

TO BE HONEST, I THOUGHT YOU'D MAKE A FUSS.
WE HIRED YOU ASSUMING IT WOULD END IN FAILURE.
THE STAR RELIGIOUS GROUP STARTED IN THE NARA PERIOD AS MASTER TENGEN WAS SPREADING JAPANESE BUDDHISM AND PREACHING THE MORAL FOUNDATION OF THE JUJUTSU SORCERERS.
HOWEVER, THE WORLDS OF JUJUTSU AND RELIGION DID NOT SEE EYE TO EYE.
FROM THAT DISPARITY, THE TIME VESSEL ASSOCIATION WAS BORN.
EVEN JUJUTSU SORCERERS WHO HAVE AUTHORIZATION BEYOND NORMAL RIGHTS FOR MANY THINGS CANNOT LAY HANDS ON NON-CURSE USERS.
AND BECAUSE OF THAT, WE POSITION OURSELVES AS NON-CURSE USERS.
THE TIME HAS COME...
...FOR THE TABOO MENTIONED IN THE DOCTRINE!
WE HAVE HELD STEADFAST TO OUR MONO-THEISM!!
AND NOW THE THREAT OF THIS IMPURE MERGER WITH MASTER TENGEN IS UPON US!!

IF THE FOLLOWERS WERE TO WITNESS SUCH A MERGER, THE ASSOCIATION WOULD CEASE TO EXIST.
HOWEVER, IF WE PUSH TOO HARD, THE SORCERERS WOULD DESTROY US.
THIS WAS AN ACT OF DESPERATION!
BUT LOOK AT US NOW!
WHAT WAS ONCE LOST IS NOW IN THE PALM OF OUR HAND.
IT'S ENOUGH TO LOOSEN OUR PURSE STRINGS.
IF IT MEANS WE FALL ALONGSIDE THE STAR, SO BE IT.
IF MASTER TENGEN GOES BERSERK...
...HUMANITY WILL BE DESTROYED. YOU KNOW THAT, RIGHT?

WHEN YOU MENTIONED THE ASSOCIATION'S HELP, DID YOU MEAN OKINAWA?
YEAH.
WHY DIDN'T YOU KILL THE MAID THEN?
I THOUGHT I TOLD YOU TO.
TAKE HER FAR AWAY...
...AND JUST KILL HER ALREADY.
BECAUSE I HAD AN IDEA OF WHAT YOUR PLAN WAS.
I'M JUST THE MIDDLEMAN. DON'T GET ME INVOLVED.
INSTEAD OF USING THE MAID'S DEATH, I FIGURED CREATING A FALSE SENSE OF SECURITY FROM A SUCCESSFUL RESCUE WOULD HELP YOU WEAR THEM DOWN.
YOU'VE NEVER BEEN SHY ABOUT APPEASING OTHERS IN ORDER TO HIDE YOUR TRUE INTENTIONS THOUGH, HAVE YOU?
ALL'S WELL THAT ENDS WELL.
WHAT WAS OKINAWA ALL ABOUT?
HILARIOUS, WASN'T IT?
YOU'D USUALLY USE A CAR TO TRANSPORT A HOSTAGE, RIGHT?
BECAUSE IT'S RISKY TRAVELING ON PUBLIC TRANSPORTATION.

THE ASSOCIATION HEAD OWNS A PRIVATE JET.
EVEN SO...
RICH PEOPLE JUST THINK DIFFERENTLY.
LET'S GRAB SOME FOOD WITH THAT MONEY.
SHOW ME A RESTAURANT YOU USE FOR BUTTERING UP YOUR CLIENTS.
FORGET IT.
YOU DON'T PLAN ON PAYING ANYWAY.
I PROMISED MYSELF THAT I'D ONLY ASSOCIATE WITH YOU...
...IN BUSINESS OR IN HELL.

YO.
LONG TIME NO SEE.
...
FOR REAL?
FOR REAL REAL.
I FEEL LIKE NEW.

REVERSE CURSED TECH-NIQUE!
TAP TAP
COR-RECT!
WHEN YOU SO KINDLY STABBED ME THROUGH MY THROAT, I GAVE UP ON FIGHT-ING BACK.
INSTEAD, I FOCUSED EVERYTHING I HAD INTO REVERSE CURSED TECHNIQUE.
CURSED ENERGY IS BORN FROM NEGATIVITY. EVEN IF YOU CAN REINFORCE YOUR BODY, RECONSTRUCTING BODY PARTS IS IMPOSSIBLE.
THAT'S WHY YOU MULTIPLY THE NEGATIVE ENERGY TOGETHER TO MAKE POSITIVE ENERGY. THAT'S REVERSE CURSED TECHNIQUE!
⊖ × ⊖ = ⊕

BUT IT'S EASIER SAID THAN DONE.
HE'S RAMBLING...
AND YOU KNOW WHAT ELSE? I'VE NEVER BEEN ABLE TO DO IT BEFORE.
IS HE DELIRIOUS?
THE ONE PERSON I KNOW WHO CAN DO IT JUST TALKS A BUNCH OF GIBBERISH TOO.
YOU JUST FWOOSH. THEN FWISH. FWOOSH AND FWISH!
DON'T YOU GET IT, LOSER?
BUT RIGHT ON THE VERGE OF DEATH, I UNDERSTOOD!
THE CORE OF CURSED ENERGY!
YOU LOST. YOU SHOULD'VE CUT MY HEAD OFF.
AND YOU DIDN'T USE THAT CURSED TOOL WHEN YOU STABBED ME IN THE HEAD.
LOST?

THE BATTLE'S JUST BE-GINNING.

WHAT?
IS THAT RIGHT? MAYBE YOU'RE RIGHT.
YOU'RE SO RIGHT!!

THE POSITIVE ENERGY BORN FROM REVERSE CURSED TECHNIQUE...
...FLOWS INTO THE LIMITLESS CURSED TECHNIQUE CARVED INTO ME.

CURSED TECHNIQUE REVERSAL
RED

ZWEEEN
KRMBL...
HEH...

YOU'RE A MONSTER!

IS THAT RIGHT?
MAYBE YOU'RE RIGHT.
YOU'RE SO RIGHT!
...
WHAT?
YOU WANTED TO USE IT THREE WAYS?

Chapter 75: Hidden Inventory, Part 11

KRK
KRK
MY BONES AREN'T BROKEN. SO THAT ENERGY WAVE (?) JUST NOW WAS RED, THE CURSED TECHNIQUE REVERSAL OF THE LIMITLESS...

① THE POWER TO STOP MOTION—THE NEUTRAL LIMITLESS.
CHK
CHK
CHK
② THE POWER TO ATTRACT—THE STRENGTHENED LIMITLESS BLUE.
AND ③ THE POWER TO REPEL—THE CURSED TECHNIQUE REVERSAL RED.
KLAK
NONE OF THEM...
FWIM
FWIM

WHOOM
...ARE A PROBLEM!
① HIS STOPPING TECHNIQUE HASN'T BEEN AN ISSUE FROM THE START.
② I CAN NULLIFY THE ATTRACTION TECHNIQUE WITH MY EXTENDED-REACH INVERTED SPEAR. EVEN MY SPEED IS EFFECTIVE.
③ AS LONG AS I DON'T MESS UP THE TIMING, I CAN USE THE INVERTED SPEAR AS A SHIELD AGAINST HIS RE-PELLING POWER.

THIS UNEASINESS...

THIS UNEASINESS...
NO...
EVERY-THING'S OKAY.

DIE!

SORRY, AMANAI.
RIGHT NOW, I'M NOT ANGRY FOR YOU.
NOR DO I FEEL VENGEFUL TOWARD ANYONE.

RIGHT NOW...
...IT'S JUST...
...THAT EVERYTHING...
...FEELS RIGHT.
THROUGHOUT HEAVEN AND EARTH...
...I ALONE AM THE HONORED ONE.

VWOOM

GWOOM

KSSSHHHHHH
INNATE TECHNIQUES THAT HAVE BEEN PASSED DOWN THROUGH THE GENERATIONS HAVE THE ADVANTAGE OF HOW-TO MANUALS.
THE DISADVANTAGE IS THAT WORD GETS OUT ABOUT THE TECHNIQUES.

YOU MUST BE FROM ONE OF THE BIG THREE SORCERER FAMILIES. MOST LIKELY ZEN'IN...
NO WONDER YOU KNEW ABOUT BLUE, RED...
...AND THE LIMITLESS.
BUT THIS...
...EVEN WITHIN THE GOJO FAMILY...
...IS KNOWN ONLY TO A FEW.
MOTION AND REVERSAL.
IT IS BORN BY COLLIDING BOTH INFINITES.
AN IMAGINARY MASS RUSHES FORTH...
HOLLOW TECHNIQUE!

PURPLE!

THIS UNEASINESS...
"I DON'T WORK FOR FREE."
THAT'S WHAT I WOULD ALWAYS SAY BEFORE MAKING A RUN FOR IT.
BUT NOW THE AWAKENED POWER OF THE LIMITLESS STANDS BEFORE ME. HE'S PROBABLY THE GREATEST SORCERER ALIVE.
I WANTED TO DISCREDIT IT. TO CRUSH IT.
THE PINNACLE OF THE JUJUTSU WORLD AND THE ZEN'IN FAMILY.
I WANTED THIS FOR SELF-AFFIRMATION.
AND I DEVIATED FROM MY TRUE SELF.

AT THAT POINT, I HAD ALREADY LOST.
I THOUGHT I HAD SET ASIDE SUCH PETTY PRIDE.

TO BE PROUD NEITHER OF MYSELF NOR OTHERS...
I CHOSE THAT PATH, DIDN'T I?
SO...
ANY LAST WORDS?
...
NOPE.

IN TWO OR THREE YEARS, MY KID WILL BE SOLD OFF TO THE ZEN'IN FAMILY.
DO AS YOU PLEASE.

CURSED TOOL

CHAIN OF A THOUSAND MILES

A mysterious chain that can keep extending as long as you don't let this end be seen.

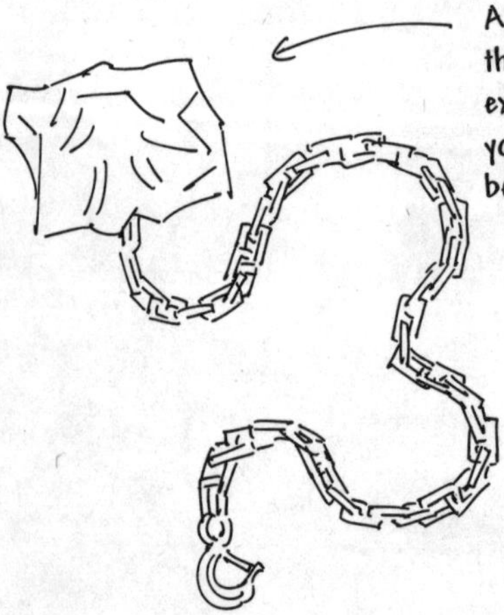

CHAPTER 76:
PREMATURE DEATH

KREAK
CLAP
CLAP
CLAP
CLAP
CLAP

YOU'RE LATE, SUGURU.
NO... I GUESS YOU'RE EARLY.
AFTER ALL, WHO KNOWS HOW MANY TIME VESSEL ASSOCIATION HIDEOUTS THERE ARE...
...
IS THAT YOU...
...SA-TORU?
WHAT HAPPENED TO YOU?!
LOOKS LIKE YOU SAW SHOKO.
YEAH, SHE FIXED ME UP. I'M FINE.

SWP
NO.
IT DOESN'T MATTER IF I'M FINE...
LET'S GET OUT OF HERE...
SUGURU.
I'M THE ONE WHO MESSED UP.
DON'T WORRY ABOUT IT.
DO YOU WANT TO...
...KILL THEM ALL?

RIGHT NOW...
...I PROBABLY WOULDN'T EVEN FEEL ANYTHING.
FORGET IT.
IT'S POINTLESS.
FROM THE LOOKS OF IT, THERE ARE ONLY FOLLOWERS OF THE FAITH HERE.
THE ONES IN CHARGE AND INVOLVED WITH THE JUJUTSU WORLD ARE PROBABLY LONG GONE.
UNLIKE WHAT HAPPENED WITH THE REWARD MONEY, THEY CAN'T TALK THEIR WAY OUT OF THIS SITUATION ANYMORE.
IT WAS A GROUP FULL OF PROBLEMS TO BEGIN WITH.
THEY'LL DISBAND IN DUE TIME.

POINT-LESS, HUH?
DOES THERE...
...NEED TO BE A REASON?
OF COURSE. IT'S IMPORTANT.
ESPECIALLY AS JUJUTSU SORCERERS.
ONE YEAR LATER

MIIIN
AUGUST 2007
MIIIN
MIIIN
MIIIN
HEADS UP!
PEN
ERASER

FWIP
SHP
TUNK

ALL RIGHT.
SHUP
ACK! WHAT WAS THAT?!
AN AUTOMATIC TARGETING OPTION FOR JUJUTSU TECHNIQUES?
YUP.
TECHNICALLY, IT'S ME THAT'S THE TARGET THOUGH.
WHAT I'D BEEN DOING MANUALLY I CAN NOW DO AUTOMATICALLY.
AND IT'S NOT JUST THE INTENSITY OF CURSED ENERGY...
...BUT ITS MASS, SPEED, SHAPE... I CAN USE THEM ALL TO DISTINGUISH THE DANGER OF THE OBJECT.
IT WOULD BE NICE TO EVENTUALLY DISTINGUISH POISONOUS OBJECTS AS WELL, BUT THAT'LL TAKE TIME.
RIGHT NOW, I CAN *ALMOST* ALWAYS KEEP THE LIMITLESS ACTIVATED AT ALL TIMES WHILE USING MINIMUM RESOURCES.

A FRESH BRAIN AT ALL TIMES.
I'LL ALSO HAVE REVERSE CURSED TECHNIQUE RUNNING AROUND THE CLOCK TO PRESERVE MYSELF.
ALWAYS?! YOU'RE GONNA FRY YOUR BRAIN!
I'VE FINALLY PERFECTED MINIMIZING THE NECESSARY HAND SIGNS.
SIMULTANEOUSLY ACTIVATING MULTIPLE *REDS* AND *BLUES* RESPECTIVELY IS COMING ALONG AS WELL.
OTHER THAN THAT, I HAVE TO WORK ON MY DOMAIN AND LONG-DISTANCE TELEPORTATION TECHNIQUES.
IF A COURSE TO THE SCHOOL WITH-OUT OBSTACLES IS SECURED IN ADVANCE, I THINK IT MIGHT BE POSSIBLE.
SHOKO, LEMME BORROW ONE OF YOUR LAB RATS.
FOR REAL?
SATORU BECAME "THE STRONGEST."

SUGURU, HAVE YOU LOST SOME WEIGHT?
YOU OKAY?
HE CAN HANDLE MISSIONS ON HIS OWN NOW.
SHOKO NEVER WENT ON DANGEROUS MISSIONS TO BEGIN WITH...
...SO BY DEFAULT, I'VE BEEN GOING ON MORE MISSIONS ALONE AS WELL.
JUST A LITTLE TIRED FROM THE SUMMER HEAT.
IT'S NOT A PROBLEM.
MAYBE YOU HAD TOO MUCH SOMEN NOODLES?
IT WAS A BUSY SUMMER.
LAST YEAR'S FREQUENT DISASTERS PROBABLY HAD SOMETHING TO DO WITH IT.
CURSES SPAWNED FROM EVERY-WHERE LIKE MAGGOTS.

AN ENDLESS CYCLE OF EXORCISM AND CONSUMPTION.
EXORCISE.
CONSUME.

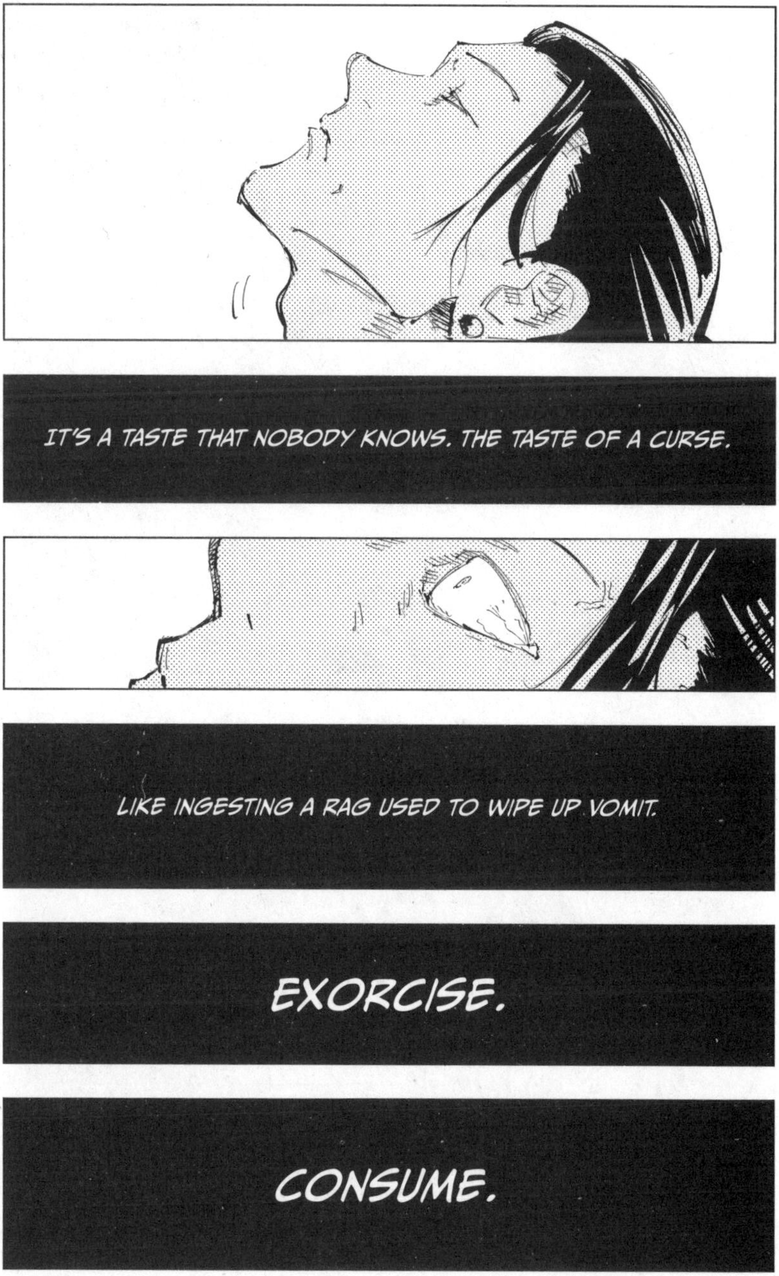
IT'S A TASTE THAT NOBODY KNOWS. THE TASTE OF A CURSE.
LIKE INGESTING A RAG USED TO WIPE UP VOMIT.
EXORCISE.
CONSUME.

FOR WHOM?
EVER SINCE THAT DAY...
...IT'S BEEN RUNNING THROUGH MY HEAD.
WHAT I SAW WAS NOTHING OUT OF THE ORDINARY.
A HIDEOUS EVIL, KNOWN TO EVERYONE.
KNOWING THAT FULL WELL...
...I CHOSE TO PROTECT THEM AS A JUJUTSU SORCERER.
FSHHHH...
DON'T LOSE YOUR WAY.

FOLLOW THROUGH WITH YOUR DUTY AS A JUJUTSU SORCERER.
SKWEAK
MONKEYS...

HI! MR. GETO!
HAIBARA...
FWIN
HOPE ALL IS WELL!
WHAT CAN I GET YOU TO DRINK?
WHAT?! NO, I COULDN'T POSSIBLY ...
I'LL TAKE A COKE!!!
HEH HEH...

MY MISSION TOMORROW IS PRETTY FAR AWAY.
THAT SO? I'LL BE EXPECTING A SOUVENIR THEN.
YOU GOT IT!! SOMETHING SWEET OR SAVORY?
SATORU WILL PROBABLY HAVE SOME TOO, SO MAYBE SOMETHING SWEET.
...
HAIBARA.
ARE YOU OKAY WITH BEING A JUJUTSU SORCERER?
DOESN'T IT BOTHER YOU?

HM... GOOD QUESTION.
I'M NOT REALLY THE TYPE TO THINK TOO HARD ABOUT THINGS.
GIVING MY ALL TOWARD SOMETHING I KNOW I CAN HELP WITH...
...IS A GREAT FEELING!
I SEE...
YEAH, YOU'RE RIGHT.
TAK TAK

TAK
ARE YOU GETO?
WHAT KIND OF GIRLS ARE YOU INTO?

FIRST-YEAR IJICHI

Chapter 77: Premature Death, Part 2

WHAT KIND OF GIRLS...
...ARE YOU INTO?
HM?
WHO ARE YOU?
I LIKE GIRLS WITH HEALTHY APPETITES!
I SEE...

HAIBARA...
IT'S FINE.
SHE'S NOT A BAD PERSON.
I'M A PRETTY GOOD JUDGE OF CHARACTER.
...
PRESENT COMPANY INCLUDED?
?
OF COURSE!!
...
HA HA HA!
HE WAS BEING SARCASTIC, KID.

GOTTA GO.
IS HE YOUR JUNIOR? SUCH AN HONEST AND CUTE KID.
AS A JUJUTSU SORCERER, HE SHOULDN'T BE SO TRUSTING.
AND YOU, GETO? AREN'T YOU GOING TO ANSWER MY QUESTION?
HOW ABOUT YOU ANSWER FIRST?
WHO ARE YOU?
SPECIAL-GRADE SORCERER YUKI TSUKUMO.
RING A BELL?

!
YOU'RE THE...?!
NICE! THE WHAT?
THE NO-GOOD SPECIAL GRADE WHO DOESN'T TAKE ON ANY MISSIONS...
...AND JUST BUMS AROUND OVERSEAS?
I HATE JUJUTSU HIGH!
HMPH!
SHE'S SULKING...
JUST KIDDING.
BUT I'M NOT LYING WHEN I SAY WE DON'T SEE EYE TO EYE.
WHAT THEY DO HERE IS TREAT SYMPTOMS. WHAT I WANT IS TO GET AT THE ROOT CAUSE.

THE ROOT CAUSE?
I DON'T WANT TO EXORCISE CURSES AFTER THEY APPEAR.
I WANT A WORLD WHERE CURSES DON'T EVEN EXIST.
!
HOW ABOUT ...
...A LITTLE LESSON?
TELL ME, WHAT ARE CURSES ANYWAY?
CURSES ARE CREATED WHEN CURSED ENERGY LEAKS FROM HUMANS. IT THEN GATHERS LIKE SEDIMENT AND TAKES FORM.
HUMANS
EXCELLENT.
IF THAT'S THE CASE, THERE ARE TWO WAYS TO CREATE A WORLD WHERE CURSES NO LONGER EXIST...

①ERADICATE CURSED ENERGY FROM ALL OF HUMANITY.
②TEACH HUMANS HOW TO CONTROL THEIR CURSED ENERGY.
THE FIRST ONE'S NOT A BAD IDEA.
THERE WAS A MODEL CASE FOR IT AFTER ALL.
A MODEL CASE?
SOME-ONE YOU'RE FAMILIAR WITH...
TOJI ZEN'IN.
THERE HAVE BEEN SEVERAL CASES WHERE HEAVENLY RESTRICTION HAS REDUCED A PERSON'S CURSED ENERGY TO NORMAL LEVELS.
BUT TO ERADICATE ONE'S CURSED ENERGY COMPLETELY.... I'VE SEARCHED ALL OVER THE WORLD, AND HE'S THE ONLY ONE WHO'S EVER DONE IT.

BY ELIM-INATING ALL CURSED ENERGY, HIS BODY BECAME SHARPENED TO THE POINT WHERE HE DEVELOPED A RESISTANCE TO CURSES.
DESPITE NOT HAVING CURSED ENERGY, TOJI ZEN'IN WAS ABLE TO SENSE CURSES USING HIS FIVE SENSES.
VLP LUP LUP
BUT THAT'S NOT THE ONLY THING THAT'S INTERESTING ABOUT HIM.
...
HE WAS TRULY SUPER-HUMAN.
DON'T FEEL BAD ABOUT LOSING TO HIM.
I WANTED TO RESEARCH HIM, BUT HE BLEW ME OFF.
IT'S TOO BAD HE DIED.
CASES OF HEAVENLY RESTRICTION ARE FEW AND FAR BETWEEN...
...SO MY FOCUS IS ON ②.
DID YOU KNOW...
...JUJUTSU SORCERERS DON'T GIVE BIRTH TO CURSES?
?!
OF COURSE, THAT'S EXCLUDING CASES WHERE SORCERERS BECOME CURSES AFTER DEATH.

THE AMOUNT OF CURSED ENERGY THAT LEAKS FROM SORCERERS, COMPARED TO FROM NON-SORCERERS, IS EXTREMELY LOW.
NON-SORCERER
SORCERER
THERE IS A DIFFERENCE IN HOW MUCH WE CONSUME AND USE CURSED ENERGY BECAUSE OF OUR PROFESSION.
BUT THE REAL REASON LIES IN HOW IT FLOWS THROUGH US. FOR SORCERERS, IT FLOWS HEAVILY *WITHIN* US.
IF WE'RE TALKING IN GENERAL TERMS...
...IF EVERY SINGLE HUMAN BECAME A JUJUTSU SORCER-ER...
...NO CURSE WOULD EVER BE BORN AGAIN.

THEN...
...WHY NOT JUST KILL EVERY NON-JUJUTSU SORCERER?
GETO...
THAT IS AN OPTION.

IN FACT, THAT MIGHT BE THE EASIEST ROUTE.
WHAT?
WEED OUT NON-JUJUTSU SORCERERS AND MAKE THEM ADAPT TO A JUJUTSU SORCERER-BASED SOCIETY.
UM...
IN OTHER WORDS, FORCED EVOLUTION.
KINDA LIKE HOW BIRDS GREW WINGS.
USING FEAR AND DANGER AS A CATALYST.
BUT...
I AIN'T THAT CRAZY.
DO YOU HATE NON-JUJUTSU SORCERERS...
...GETO?
I DON'T KNOW.

I USED TO THINK JUJUTSU SORCERERS EXISTED TO PROTECT NON-SORCERERS.
BUT RECENTLY, I'VE BEEN DOUBTING WHETHER NON-SORCERERS ARE WORTH FIGHTING FOR.
THE PRECIOUSNESS OF THE WEAK. THE UGLINESS OF THE WEAK.
I CAN NO LONGER TELL THE DIFFERENCE.
THE PART OF ME THAT LOOKS DOWN ON NON-SORCERERS... THE PART OF ME THAT TRIES TO RESIST THAT FEELING...
IF BEING A JUJUTSU SORCERER IS LIKE RUNNING A MARATHON, THEN THE FINISH LINE IS TOO UNCLEAR.
I DON'T KNOW HOW I REALLY FEEL.
ME NEITHER.
YOU'RE NOT AT THAT STAGE YET.

LOOKING DOWN ON NON-SORCERERS...
RESISTING THAT FEELING...
THOSE ARE JUST POSSIBILITIES YOU'VE THOUGHT OF.
WHATEVER YOUR TRUE FEELING IS...
...YOU STILL HAVE TO DECIDE.
VRMMM
I'LL SEE YA. I WAS HOPING TO SAY HI TO GOJO AS WELL.
BAD TIMING, I GUESS.
VUM VUM VUM VUM

AS FELLOW SPECIAL-GRADE SOR-CERERS...
LET'S ALL THREE OF US GET ALONG, OKAY?
I'LL SEND YOUR REGARDS TO GOJO.
OH, RIGHT. ONE LAST THING.
DON'T WORRY ABOUT WHAT HAPPENED WITH THE STAR PLASMA VESSEL.
WHETHER THERE WAS ANOTHER VESSEL...
...OR ANOTHER VESSEL WAS BORN...
WHATEVER HAPPENED, TENGEN IS STABILIZED.

...
I FIGURED.
ACK! I FORGOT TO GET HIS ANSWER!
IT WAS SUPPOSED TO BE A SIMPLE MISSION TO TAKE OUT A GRADE 2 CURSE!!
DAMMIT!
A GUARDIAN DEITY'S RELIGION... IT WAS A DEITY OF THAT AREA, SO IT ACTUALLY SHOULD HAVE BEEN A GRADE 1!

GET SOME REST FOR NOW, NANAMI.
GOJO TOOK THE MISSION.
...
WHY NOT JUST LET HIM TAKE CARE OF EVERYTHING BY HIMSELF FROM NOW ON?
IF BEING A JUJUTSU SORCERER IS LIKE RUNNING A MARATHON...

WHAT IF ALL THAT'S AT THE END OF THAT ROAD...
...IS A MOUNTAIN OF OUR FELLOW SORCERERS' CORPSES?
REPORT: SEPTEMBER 2007
□□ PREFECTURE □□ CITY (FORMERLY □ VILLAGE)
SKRCH
MISSION SUMMARY
SPIRIT KIDNAPPINGS AND ABNORMAL DEATHS WITHIN SAID VILLAGE.
THE CURSE THOUGHT TO BE RESPONSIBLE IS TO BE EXORCISED.

WHAT IS THIS?
WHEEZ
WHEEZ
[redacted] ...?
[redacted]?! (WHAT DO YOU MEAN? THESE TWO ARE RESPONSIBLE FOR THE INCIDENT, RIGHT?!)
NO, THEY ARE NOT.
[redacted]!! (THESE TWO POSSESS STRANGE POWERS AND OFTEN ATTACK THE VILLAGERS.)
I ALREADY DEALT WITH THE CAUSE FOR THE INCIDENT.
[redacted]!! (MY GRANDCHILD NEARLY DIED BECAUSE OF THESE TWO.)

THAT WAS BECAUSE THEY...
■■■!! (SHUT UP, YOU MONSTERS!)
■■!! (YOUR PARENTS WERE THE SAME.)
■■■!! (I KNEW WE SHOULD'VE KILLED YOU WHEN YOU WERE BORN.)
I- IT'LL... ...BE OKAY...
VWN VWN...
THE PART OF YOU THAT LOOKS DOWN ON NON-SORCERERS...
THE PART OF YOU THAT TRIES RESIST THAT FEELING...
WHATEVER YOUR TRUE FEELING IS...
LET'S...
...STEP OUTSIDE FOR A MOMENT, SHALL WE?

YOU HAVE TO BE THE ONE TO DECIDE.
AGH!
WHAT?!
WHY?!
HUH?
GYAA!
PLEASE!
NO MORE!

• FIVE DAYS AFTER DISPATCHING THE PERSON IN CHARGE (JUJUTSU HIGH THIRD-YEAR SUGURU GETO), 112 RESIDENTS OF THE FORMER VILLAGE [redacted] WERE FOUND DEAD.
• INITIALLY THOUGHT TO BE CAUSED BY THE CURSE, FURTHER INSPECTION DISCOVERED RESIDUALS BELONGING TO SUGURU GETO'S CURSE MANIPULATION TECHNIQUE.
• SUGURU GETO FLED. IN ACCORDANCE TO ARTICLE 9 OF THE JUJUTSU REGULATIONS, HE IS NOW CONSIDERED A CURSE USER AND SUBJECT TO EXECUTION.

YU HAIBARA

- He doesn't come from a family of jujutsu sorcerers, but he does have a younger sister who can see curses.
- He sternly forbid his sister from going to Jujutsu High.
- He likes rice. He likes people.

CHAPTER 78:
PREMATURE DEATH, PART 3
WHAT?
SUGURU FLED AFTER KILLING EVERYONE IN THE VILLAGE.
DON'T MAKE ME SAY IT AGAIN...

I HEARD YOU.
THAT'S WHY I SAID, "WHAT?"
...
SUGURU'S PARENTS' HOME IS VACANT AS WELL.
HOWEVER, FROM THE BLOOD-STAINS AND RESIDUALS...
...IT SEEMS HE MIGHT HAVE DONE THE SAME TO HIS PARENTS.
THERE'S NO WAY!!
SATORU.
I ALSO...
...HAVE NO IDEA WHAT THE HELL IS GOING ON...

NNNGH!
SMOKING
AREA
UM...
IS SHE A HIGH SCHOOLER?
NEED A LIGHT?

HEY!
IF IT ISN'T THE CULPRIT HIMSELF.
WHAT DO YOU WANT?
YOU COULD SAY I'M TESTING MY LUCK.
I SEE...
I'LL ASK FOR THE HELL OF IT— ARE THESE ACCUSATIONS AGAINST YOU FALSE?
NO, I'M AFRAID NOT.

ANOTHER ONE FOR YA...
WHY'D YOU DO IT?
I'M GOING TO CREATE A WORLD OF ONLY JUJUTSU SORCERERS.
HA HA HA!
WHAT THE HECK DOES THAT MEAN?
I'M NOT A CHILD ANYMORE.
I DON'T NEED EVERYONE TO UNDERSTAND.
SULKING BECAUSE NO ONE UNDERSTANDS YOU...
SOUNDS AWFULLY CHILDISH IF YOU ASK ME.
HEY, GOJO?

GETO'S HERE.
YEAH. IN SHINJUKU.
NO WAY. I DON'T WANNA BE KILLED.

EXPLAIN YOURSELF...
...SUGURU!
YOU ALREADY HEARD FROM SHOKO, DIDN'T YOU?
THAT'S ALL THERE IS TO IT.
THAT'S REASON ENOUGH FOR YOU TO KILL ALL NON-SORCERERS?!
EVEN YOUR PARENTS?!

IT WOULDN'T BE FAIR IF I MADE AN EXCEPTION FOR MY PARENTS, WOULD IT?
BESIDES, MY FAMILY NOW CONSISTS OF MORE THAN JUST THEM.
THAT'S NOT WHAT I'M TALKING ABOUT.
YOU WERE THE ONE WHO SAID KILLING NON-SORCERERS IS POINTLESS.
THERE IS A POINT AND A MEANING TO IT.
IT'S ALSO JUSTICE.
NO WAY!
KILLING ALL NON-SORCERERS TO MAKE A WORLD OF ONLY SORCERERS?!
THAT'S IMPOSSIBLE!!
AND THERE'S NO POINT...
...IN ATTEMPTING THE IMPOSSIBLE!!
...
HOW ARROGANT.
WHAT?!

YOU COULD DO IT...
...SATORU.
YOU'RE TRYING TO CONVINCE ME THAT IT'S IMPOSSIBLE...
...WHEN YOU YOURSELF COULD DO IT.
ARE YOU THE STRONGEST BECAUSE YOU'RE SATORU GOJO?
OR ARE YOU SATORU GOJO BECAUSE YOU'RE THE STRONGEST?

WHAT'RE YOU GETTING AT?!
IF I COULD BE YOU...
...WOULDN'T MY IMPOS-SIBLE IDEAL BECOME POSSIBLE?
THIS IS THE LIFE I'VE CHOSEN.
ALL I CAN DO NOW IS GIVE IT ALL I'VE GOT.
VOON

IF YOU WANT TO KILL ME, KILL ME.
THERE'S MEANING IN THAT TOO.

WHY DID YOU LET HIM GO?
...
ARE YOU... REALLY ASKING ME THAT?
NO, YOU'RE RIGHT...
I'M SORRY.
SEN-SEI.
I'M STRONG, RIGHT?
YEAH.
IN THE IMPUDENCE DEPARTMENT TOO.

IT LOOKS LIKE JUST BEING STRONG ISN'T ENOUGH.
BUT...
I CAN ONLY SAVE THOSE...
...WHO ARE PREPARED TO BE SAVED.
I THOUGHT THE STAR RELIGIOUS GROUP HAD DISBANDED?
THERE ARE OTHER GROUPS WITH SIMILAR IDEALS.

IT STILL LOOKS LIKE A RELIGIOUS GROUP TO THE PUBLIC. ARE YOU OKAY WITH THAT?
AS LONG AS I CAN COLLECT CURSES AND MONEY, THAT'S ALL RIGHT.
ARE YOU REALLY GOING OUT THERE LOOKING LIKE THAT?
WHY NOT? BLUFFING AND LOOKING THE PART IS IMPORTANT.
MASTER GETO...
BE SURE TO WATCH CLOSELY.
HAVE THEY GATHERED?
DIRECTORS. REPRESENT-ATIVES. THE CHAIRMAN.
AND A LOT MORE MONEY WAITING.

KREEN
DUN BOP
CAN EVERYONE HEAR ME? THANK YOU FOR WAITING. I'LL KEEP THIS SHORT.

AS OF THIS MOMENT, THIS GROUP IS MINE.
WE'LL HAVE A NEW NAME AS WELL. YOU WILL ALL OBEY ME.
NUMEROUS VOICES RISE IN OPPOSITION.
WELL ISN'T THAT A SHAME.
I GOT IT!
MR. SONODA! COULD YOU PLEASE COME UP TO THE STAGE?
THAT'S RIGHT! YOU!

GRRUNCH
VONK
DUN DUN
NOW THEN...
LET'S TRY AGAIN.

OBEY.
ME.
MONKEYS.
I DON'T LIKE MONKEYS. THAT'S THE TRUTH I CHOSE.

MEGUMI...
...FUSHI-GURO, RIGHT?
WHO'RE YOU?
AND...
WHY'RE YOU LOOKING AT ME LIKE THAT?
WELL, IT'S JUST... YOU LOOK EXACTLY LIKE HIM.
?

공 서우

SHIU KONG

- He's a Korean citizen.
- He's a former detective.
- Akutami thinks he is the coolest one in the backstory.

Chapter 79: A Taste of Things to Come

SO, YOUR DAD IS ACTUALLY FROM THE REPUTABLE ZEN'IN SORCERER FAMILY.
EVEN I THINK HE'S JUST A BIG LOSER. HE LEFT THE FAMILY AND HAD YOU.
YOU HAVE POWERS, AND YOU CAN SEE THEM, RIGHT?
I BET YOU'VE ALREADY MANIFESTED YOUR CURSED TECHNIQUE TOO.
THE ZEN'IN FAMILY LOVES SORCERERS BLESSED WITH QUALITY CURSED POWER!
A CURSED TECHNIQUE TYPICALLY MANIFESTS BETWEEN THE AGES OF FOUR AND SIX.
A RIPE TIME TO SELL!
YOUR DAD KEPT YOU HIDDEN FROM THE ZEN'IN FAMILY.
HIS TRUMP CARD.
¥

SUCKS, DOESN'T IT?
YOUR DAD... I KI—
SO WHAT?
I DON'T CARE WHERE HE IS OR WHAT HE'S DOING.
I HAVEN'T SEEN HIM IN YEARS. I DON'T EVEN REMEMBER WHAT HE LOOKS LIKE.
BUT I GET THE GIST OF WHAT YOU'RE TALKING ABOUT.
TSUMIKI'S MOM HASN'T RETURNED IN A WHILE EITHER.
HEY, MEGUMI'S BACK.
SO THAT MEANS THEY'RE DONE TAKING CARE OF US...
...AND ARE LIVING HAPPILY TOGETHER.
ARE YOU REALLY A FIRST GRADER?

WELL, IF YOU EVER GET CURIOUS ABOUT YOUR DAD, JUST ASK.
HUP
I THINK YOU MIGHT FIND IT INTERESTING.
NOW THEN, LET'S GET DOWN TO BUSINESS.
WHAT DO YOU WANT TO DO?
DO YOU WANT TO GO TO THE ZEN'IN FAMILY?
WHAT'LL HAPPEN TO TSUMIKI?
IF WE GO THERE, WILL TSUMIKI BE HAPPY?
MY ANSWER DEPENDS ON THAT.
NO.
THERE'S ABSO-LUTELY NO WAY.
I GUAR-ANTEE THAT.

GRK
HEH HEH...
GOTCHA!
I'LL TAKE CARE OF THINGS!
BUT YOU'RE GONNA HAVE TO WORK EXTRA HARD.
I'M COUNTIN' ON YA.

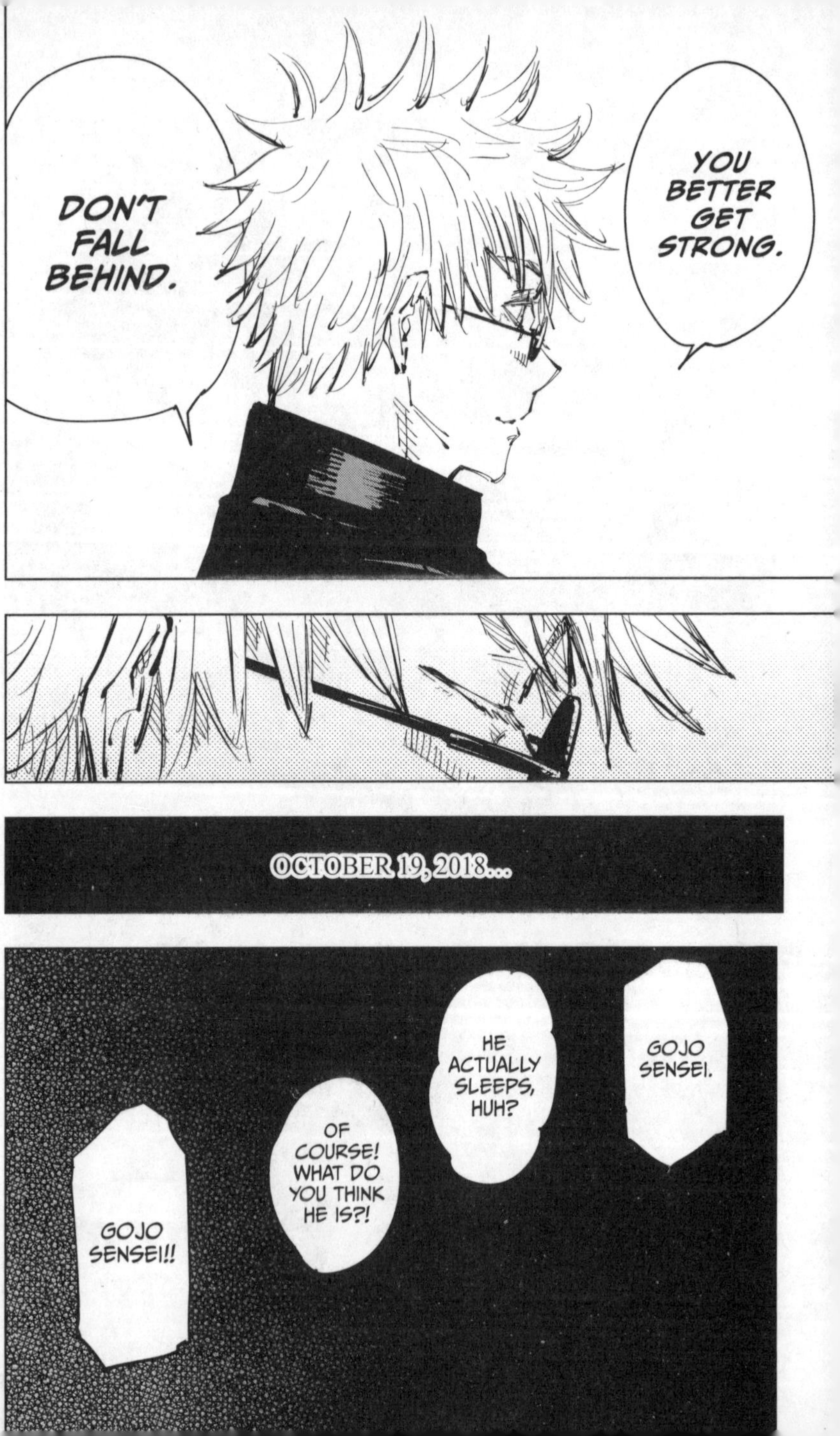
YOU BETTER GET STRONG.
DON'T FALL BEHIND.
OCTOBER 19, 2018...
GOJO SENSEI.
HE ACTUALLY SLEEPS, HUH?
OF COURSE! WHAT DO YOU THINK HE IS?!
GOJO SENSEI!!

HEY.
HE'S UP.
WAIT A SECOND. THAT'S AN EXPENSIVE CHAIR, ISN'T IT?!
YOU'RE THE ONE WHO CALLED US HERE. PLEASE DON'T GO DOZING OFF.

WHAT'RE YOU SMILING ABOUT?
OH, NOTHING. ♡
FWSHHH...

THIS WAY, PLEASE.
GOJO HAS INFORMED YOU ALL ABOUT THE MOLE, RIGHT?
YES.
WE THINK THERE'RE TWO OR MORE PEOPLE FEEDING INTEL TO THE CURSE USERS.
ONE HAS TO BE HIGHLY RANKED, EVEN HIGHER THAN THE PRINCIPALS. I CAN'T DO ANYTHING ABOUT THAT.
THE OTHER IS SOMEONE FEEDING INFORMATION TO THAT HIGHER-UP...
TODAY'S TARGET.
THEY'RE STILL ONLY UNDER SUSPICION...
...SO AFTER APPREHENDING THE SUSPECT, WE NEED TO CONDUCT AN INTER-ROGATION.

SO...
IT'S SOMEONE FROM THE KYOTO SCHOOL, RIGHT?
WHOA!
IT HAS TO BE, SINCE YOU CONFIDED WITH US FROM THE TOKYO BRANCH.
WOW, KUGI-SAKI...
...
THE MOLE IS...
MIWA!
MECHA-MARUUU!

THERE YOU ARE.
NOTE-BOOKS ARE DUE TODAY.
...
MECHA-MARU?
SORRY, MIWA. I'M GONNA SLEEP FOR A BIT.
MY NOTE-BOOK'S ON THE DESK.
SLEEP? BUT IT'S STILL EARLY...
...
SHEESH...

TNK
TNK
HE'S ACTUALLY SLEEPING.
I WONDER WHERE THE REAL MECHAMARU IS...
THE REAL MECHAMARU, KOKICHI MUTA, IS DOWN HERE.
WE DON'T SUSPECT HIM BECAUSE HE'S SUSPICIOUS—WE CAME TO THAT CONCLUSION BY PROCESS OF ELIMINATION.
PUPPET MANIPULATION...
ITS RANGE, THANKS TO HIS HEAVENLY RESTRICTION, REACHES THE ENTIRE NATION.
USING UNREGISTERED PUPPETS THAT ACT AS MOLES TO STEAL INFORMATION WOULD BE EASY FOR HIM.
REALLY? BUT IT'D DRAW A LOT OF ATTENTION IF YOU ASK ME.

WHAT IF THE PUPPET WAS AS SMALL AS A FLY OR MOSQUITO?
HERE.
OH, YEAH.
THAT'S POSSIBLE.
...
SO, YOU'VE COME.
VOON VOON VOON...

GR
AK
!!
UM...
HE GOT US.

SO THIS MEANS...
IT'S CONFIRMED. MECHAMARU'S THE MOLE.
YOU SURE TOOK YOUR TIME.
I WAS BEGINNING TO THINK YOU FORGOT ABOUT ME.
WE WOULDN'T DARE.

THE CONSEQUENCES OF CURSED RESTRICTION ARE SOMETHING YOU KNOW BETTER THAN ANYONE.
YEESH! AS ALWAYS ...
IT STINKS OF MOLD.
HE'S OUR ENEMY NOW. LET'S JUST KILL HIM ALREADY.
NOT YET, MAHITO.
WE AGREED TO HEAL HIS BODY WITH YOUR IDLE TRANSFIGURATION...
...IN EXCHANGE FOR COOPERATION AND INFORMATION.
WE'VE MADE THIS BINDING VOW WITH HIM.
THE KILLING PART COMES AFTER YOU FIX HIM UP.

IT WOULD'VE BEEN GREAT TO HAVE USED HIM IN SHIBUYA...
OH WELL...
"DON'T LAY A FINGER ON ANYONE FROM KYOTO JUJUTSU HIGH."
YOU'RE THE ONES WHO BROKE THE BINDING VOW FIRST.
BUT THAT WAS HANAMI...
DON'T PIN THAT ON US!
I'M NOT HERE TO ARGUE OVER DETAILS WITH A CURSE.
HURRY UP AND HEAL ME...
...YOU SCUM.

DON'T BLAME ME IF I TURN YOU INTO A CATER-PILLAR.
MAHITO.
A BINDING VOW MADE WITH ANOTHER PERSON...
...IS A WHOLE DIFFERENT BEAST THAN A BINDING VOW IMPOSED ON ONESELF.
ONE OF THE DIFFER-ENCES...
...IS THAT THE "PENALTY" IS UNKNOWN.
WHEN BREAKING A BINDING VOW WITH ONESELF...
...THE WORST THAT CAN HAPPEN IS LOSING WHAT WAS GAINED.
WE CAN'T TAKE THAT RISK.
IF WE BREAK THE BINDING VOW NOW, WHO KNOWS WHEN AND WHAT SORT OF RETRIBUTION MIGHT COME OUR WAY.
YEAH, YEAH.

YOU BETTER BE THANKFUL.
YOU'RE EVEN LOWER THAN SCUM.
VWOON
IDLE TRANSFIGU-RATION

KRK KRK
KRK KRK
GRK GRK
BOO-ORING.
HOW ABOUT SHOWING SOME ENTHUSIASM?
THAT...
...COMES AFTER WE SETTLE OUR BUSINESS.
...
TRUE.
WELL, THEN...

LET'S BEGIN!
TO BE CONTINUED

TOJI FUSHIGURO

• He doesn't have much money, so he wanders from woman to woman. But he'll earn a ton of money from one job and spend it until it's gone.

• He became unstable while with the Zen'in household, but calmed down thanks to Megumi-mama. However, she died soon after Megumi was born, so Toji ended up like this.

• He can fight effectively against jujutsu sorcerers even without cursed tools. However, he can't exorcise cursed spirits. Because of this, he was ostracized by the Zen'in family.

JUJUTSU KAISEN reads from right to left, starting in the upper-right corner. Japanese is read from right to left, meaning that action, sound effects and word-balloon order are completely reversed from English order.

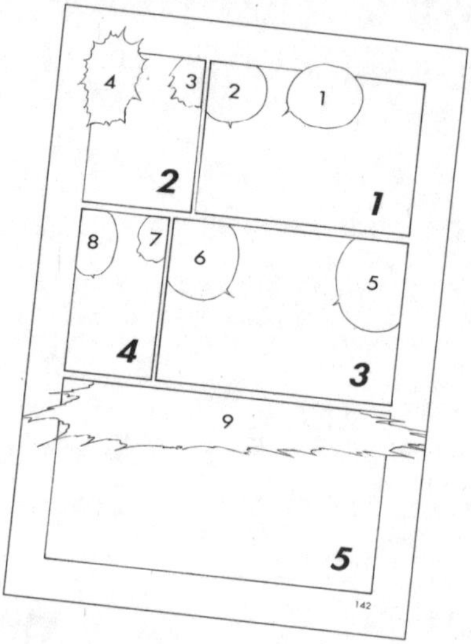